A Child's Day In...

My Life in
INDONESIA

Alex Woolf

W
FRANKLIN WATTS
LONDON • SYDNEY

First published in 2015 by Franklin Watts

Copyright © Arcturus Holdings Limited

Franklin Watts
338 Euston Road
London
NW1 3BH

Franklin Watts Australia
Level 17/207 Kent Street, Sydney, NSW 2000

Produced by Arcturus Publishing Limited,
26/27 Bickels Yard, 151–153 Bermondsey Street, London SE1 3HA

Editor: Joe Harris
Designer: Ian Winton

Picture credits:
All photography courtesy of Denny Pohan/Demotix/Corbis.

A CIP catalogue record for this book is available from the British Library.

Dewey Decimal Classification Number: 959.8'042

ISBN: 978 1 4451 3739 1

Franklin Watts is a division of Hachette Children's Books, an Hachette UK company.
www.hachette.co.uk

Printed in China

SL004302UK

Supplier 03, Date 1014, Print Run 3569

Contents

Morning

Hello! My name is Eva. I am ten years old and I live with my mother and father in Soya, a town in Indonesia.

Every morning I get up very early and collect water from the tank for my shower.

We have a water tank next to our house. We use this water for cooking, cleaning and washing. Water must be boiled to make it safe for drinking.

I get dressed in my school uniform. Then I brush my teeth and comb my hair.

Eva says ...

I wear a white and red school uniform, which is typical here in Indonesia.

My country

The Republic of Indonesia is a country of over 17,500 islands in South-East Asia and Oceania. I live on the island of Ambon.

5

Breakfast

Mum calls me for breakfast at 6 o'clock. She ate earlier, because she has to get ready for work. Dad has already left to open the family shop. So I eat on my own.

Mum boils water for our breakfast. She makes us rice with fried tempeh and mie goreng.

Tempeh is a traditional food of Indonesia, made from soybeans. It tastes delicious fried.

Mie goreng is Chinese noodles. It is made with thin yellow noodles fried with oil, garlic, meat and vegetables.

Eva says ...

Rice and tempeh are quite enough for me!

Indonesian food

In my country, we have rice with almost every meal. We might have it with meat or vegetables, and sometimes soup.

Walking to school

At 6.30, I leave for school. By this time Mum has already taken the bus to Ambon City where she works as a civil servant.

Eva says ...
Mornings are always such a rush!

Soya lies at the foot of the beautiful Sirimau Mountain, which is covered in ancient trees. From the top there are spectacular views of the bay and Ambon City.

When Dad isn't working in the family shop, he does gardening in the neighbourhood.

It's a 15-minute walk up and down hills. I usually see my friends and walk with them.

Ambon Island

The island where we live is part of the Maluku Islands in eastern Indonesia. It is green and mountainous. The main city is also called Ambon.

Morning register

My school is called Soya Kota Ambon. In my country, children start school at six years old. I am in the fourth grade.

The bell is rung at 7 o'clock for the start of school.

Elementary school is called *Sekolah Dasar*. The school year starts in mid-July and finishes in mid-June. We get two weeks holiday in December.

10

Eva says ...
We must answer 'Yes!' in a loud voice when the teacher calls out our names.

After doing the register, our teacher leads us in morning worship.

School

Next year is my last year at elementary school. After that, I will go to junior secondary school, and I will stay there until I am 14.

Lesson time

Lessons begin at 7.30 and each one lasts about 40 minutes. The teachers are quite strict, but we still manage to have some fun during class.

Eva says ...
Here I am with some of my classmates.

I am studying 11 subjects at school. My favourites are natural science, maths and cultural arts and skills.

When I started at school, I was allowed to speak my mother tongue, Ambonese. But since Grade 3 we have always had to speak in Indonesian.

Time to get to work! These maths problems are pretty tough.

Many languages

Indonesia is a country of over 700 languages. Indonesian (which we call Bahasa Indonesia) is the official language, but most of us speak our mother tongue at home.

Physical education

At 10.00, we have a break from classroom lessons and do physical education. Everyone must do PE. It's part of the curriculum.

Eva says ...

PE can be tiring, but at least we're outside.

Since I began Grade 4, we've started to do different sports, such as badminton, tennis, soccer, futsal, rounders and basketball.

Sepak Takraw is another popular sport here. It's like volleyball, but players use their feet, knees, chest and head to touch the ball, not their hands.

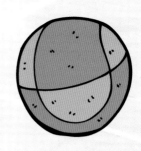

We are practising Pencak Silat, a traditional dance and martial art of Indonesia.

Sport

Indonesians are mad about badminton. We have won many Olympic gold medals in this sport. Football is also very popular.

Playtime and lunch

After some more classroom lessons, we take a break. We go out into the playground for half an hour. At 12.30, the bell goes for lunch.

Eva says ...

My best friend at school is Meiliani.

It is sunny outside. Because we are near the equator, we have a tropical climate. It is warm all year round. The rainy season lasts from November to March.

I enjoy skipping, but I'm not that good at it!

For lunch, we are served nasi uduk (rice cooked in coconut milk) and salad.

Petak benteng

In this Indonesian playground game, there are two teams and each must defend their 'fort' (it could be anything, like a bench or a tree) and at the same time try and capture the other team's fort.

Traditional dancing

At 2 o'clock, we move aside the desks and chairs to create some space so we can practise traditional Indonesian dancing.

Eva says ...

The dances are complicated. It's not easy to remember all the steps.

My country is made up of many different ethnic groups and they all have their dances. In fact there are more than 3,000 traditional dances in Indonesia.

Here we are practising a traditional court dance.

This is the maluku. Dancing around bamboo poles is fun, but you have to be careful not to trip up!

Indonesian dance

Our culture has many kinds of dance, from ancient tribal dances to religious and folk dances. The costumes can be spectacular!

Hometime

School ends at 3 o'clock. I go home, change out of my uniform and take my bike for a ride.

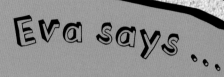

Eva says ...

I love cycling around the streets of my town – except for the uphill parts!

I go to school six days a week, and this is always my favourite time of day. I like to play games with my friends.

Sometimes we play a skipping game called *lompat tali*, in which we take turns to jump over an elastic rope. Or we might play *bekel*, a game similar to jacks.

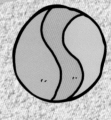

Today we're playing *kereleng* (marbles). I'm trying to knock the marble out of the circle.

Kite flying

On windy days, we go *layang-layang* – kite flying. We make our kites from bamboo, waxed paper and string.

21

Music practice

My game is cut short, because I must go back home and do my flute practice. I started playing last year and my teacher says I must practise every day.

Eva says ...
I play an Indian eight-hole bamboo flute.

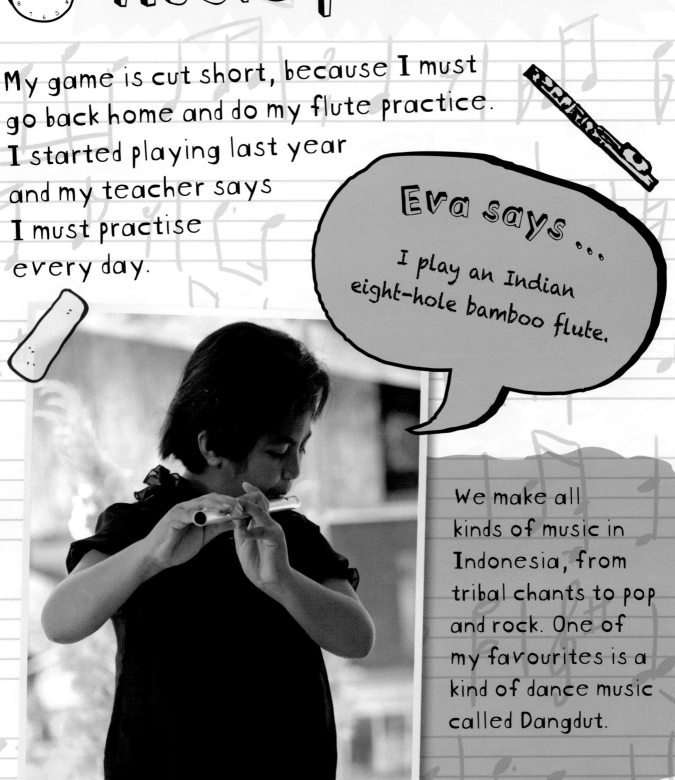

We make all kinds of music in Indonesia, from tribal chants to pop and rock. One of my favourites is a kind of dance music called Dangdut.

Most Indonesians are Muslim, but my family is Christian. Every Sunday, I sing in the church choir. This evening is choir practice, so I must hurry to church.

We are practising some hymns. I love it when we sing harmonies.

Gamelan

Our most famous music is probably *gamelan*, which uses drums, gongs, metallophones, bamboo flutes and sometimes singers.

Family shop

At 5.30, I head over to the family shop to close it up for the evening. It is in the high street, not far from our house.

Eva says ...

I check how much stock we have of the most popular products, then list the ones we're running out of.

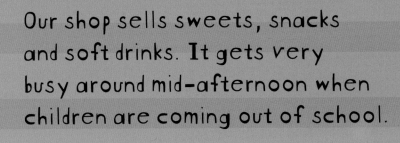

Our shop sells sweets, snacks and soft drinks. It gets very busy around mid-afternoon when children are coming out of school.

24

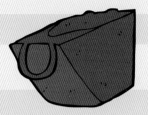

The high street is always a lively place, with street vendors selling hot snacks and *becaks* (bicycle rickshaws) taking people from place to place.

I lock the door carefully and close the shutters to stop anyone breaking in.

Indonesian money

We call our currency the *rupiah*. Sometimes we call it *perak* (silver), as a nickname. There are about 19,000 *rupiah* to a British pound [11,000 to a US dollar].

6.30 PM

At home

When I get back home from the shop, I do my homework. This evening, I must practise writing English sentences.

Eva says ...
Writing in English is very hard!

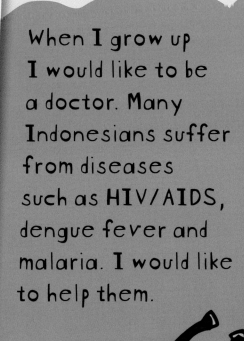

When I grow up I would like to be a doctor. Many Indonesians suffer from diseases such as HIV/AIDS, dengue fever and malaria. I would like to help them.

26

My aunt works as a nurse in the hospital in Ambon City. She says that unsafe drinking water is a major cause of death in young children. We always boil ours.

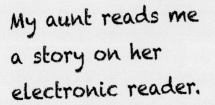

My aunt reads me a story on her electronic reader.

My Plans

When I'm 14 I want to go to a senior secondary school specialising in science and medicine. After that, I hope to go to medical school. The nearest one to Ambon is in Makassar.

Evening meal

At half past seven, we sit down to eat a meal of rice, noodles and dried fish. We talk about what we did today.

Eva says ...

My aunt and cousin join us for the meal.

Mum fried the dried fish with peanuts. This dish is called *teri kacang*, and it is originally from Java.

I'm very hungry after having such an active day!

After we finish eating, I help Mum wash the dishes, then I get ready to go to bed. It's about 8 o'clock by now and I'm very sleepy. Goodnight!

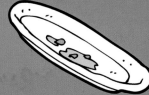

Tumpeng

When we celebrate a family birthday, we have a *slametan*, or feast. And we cook *tumpeng*, which is a cone-shaped mound of rice surrounded by other dishes.

Glossary

civil servant Someone who works for the government, helping to deliver public services.

climate The weather conditions found in a particular place over a long period of time.

cultural Relating to the arts and achievements of a particular people or nation.

curriculum The subjects that must be studied.

dengue fever A disease of the tropics, caught from mosquitoes. It causes sudden fever and acute pain in the joints.

ethnic groups A group with its own national or cultural traditions.

futsal A form of football played with five players per side on a smaller, usually indoor, pitch.

HIV/AIDS HIV (human immunodeficiency virus) is a virus that can lead to the disease AIDS (acquired immunodeficiency syndrome), which lowers the body's resistance to infection.

Java An island in Indonesia, Java is the world's most populous island with a population of 143 million (2014). The country's capital, Jakarta, is on Java.

malaria A disease of the tropics, transmitted by mosquitoes. It invades the red blood cells. It causes fever, headache, and, in severe cases, death.

metallophones A musical instrument in which the sound is produced by striking metal bars of varying pitches.

mother tongue The language a person has grown up speaking from early childhood.

Oceania An area that covers the islands of the Pacific Ocean and neighbouring seas.

soybeans Plants native to Asia, which are grown for their beans.

street vendors People who sell things in the street, either from a stall or van or with their goods laid out on the pavement.

Further information

Websites

www.ducksters.com/geography/country.php?country=Indonesia
  A single-page profile of Indonesia, full of useful facts.

kids.embassyofindonesia.org/aboutIndonesiacover.htm
  A general introduction to Indonesia, produced by the Indonesian
  Embassy in the United States, with information about the country's
  people, history, geography, language and wildlife.

kidworldcitizen.org/2013/06/23/kids-learn-about-indonesia/
  An interesting blog about Indonesia.

www.infoplease.com/country/indonesia.html?pageno=1
  Information about Indonesia's history.

www.timeforkids.com/destination/indonesia
  Facts about Indonesia, including a sightseeing guide, Indonesian
  phrases and a day in the life of a typical Indonesian child.

Further reading

All About Indonesia: Stories, Songs and Crafts for Kids by Linda Hibbs
  (Tuttle, 2014)

I is for Indonesia (Alphabetic World) by Elizabeth Rush and Eddie Hara
  (ThingsAsian Press, 2013)

Spotlight on Indonesia (Spotlight on My Country) by Bobbie Kalman
  (Crabtree, 2010)

We Visit Indonesia (Your Land and My Land: Asia) by Russell Roberts
  (Mitchell Lane, 2014)

Welcome to Indonesia (Welcome to the World) by Patrick Ryan
  (Child's World, 2007)

Index

Series contents

A Child's Day In...

My Life in BRAZIL

• Waking up • Getting dressed • Walking to school • Lessons begin • Break time • Back to work! • Lunchtime • More lessons • School's out • Helping at home • Downtime • Hobbies • Dinner and bedtime

My Life in FRANCE

• My day begins • Going to school • Registration • Morning classes • Maths lesson • Lunchtime • Back to school • Afternoon classes • Homework • Baking a cake • Music practice • Playtime • Dinner and bedtime

My Life in INDIA

• Morning • Getting ready • Going to school • School assembly • Lessons • Art and music • Sport • Hometime • Lunch • Out and about • Shopping • At home • Evening meal

My Life in INDONESIA

• Morning • Breakfast • Walking to school • Morning register • Lesson time • Physical education • Playtime and lunch • Traditional dancing • Hometime • Music practice • Family shop • At home • Evening meal

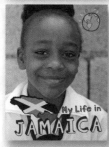

My Life in JAMAICA

• My home • Breakfast • Time to go • The school bus • My school • Lessons begin • Break time • Maths class • Lunchtime • Afternoon lessons • Dance class • Shopping • Dinner and bedtime

My Life in KENYA

• Getting up • Breakfast • Walking to school • Lesson time • Playtime • In the library • Eating lunch • Afternoon lessons • Walking home • Fetching water • At the market • Evening meal • Going to bed